EXPANSION

THE LEWIS AND CLARK EXPEDITION

by Blythe Lawrence

FOCUS READERS

WWW.FOCUSREADERS.COM

Focus Readers is distributed by North Star Editions:
sales@northstareditions.com | 888-417-0195

Produced for Focus Readers by Red Line Editorial.

Content Consultant: Dr. Gideon Mailer, Associate Professor of History, University of Minnesota Duluth

Photographs ©: Everett Historical/Shutterstock Images, cover, 1; North Wind Picture Archives, 4–5, 13, 18–19, 28; Red Line Editorial, 7, 23; IanDagnall Computing/Alamy, 9; Ival Lawhon Jr./St. Joseph News-Press/AP Images, 10–11; Angel Wynn/Danita Delimont/Alamy, 14, 17; Bettmann/Getty Images, 20; Pictorial Press Ltd/Alamy, 22; Paul Richard Jones/Shutterstock Images, 24–25; Krasnova Ekaterina/Shutterstock Images, 26

ISBN
978-1-63517-882-1 (hardcover)
978-1-63517-983-5 (paperback)
978-1-64185-186-2 (ebook pdf)
978-1-64185-085-8 (hosted ebook)

Library of Congress Control Number: 2018931649

Printed in the United States of America
Mankato, MN
May, 2018

ABOUT THE AUTHOR
Blythe Lawrence is a journalist from Seattle.

TABLE OF CONTENTS

CHAPTER 1

BEYOND THE MISSISSIPPI

In the early 1800s, settlers began moving to the western part of the United States. But most settlers did not cross the Mississippi River. West of this river was a large **territory** known as Louisiana.

This territory belonged to France. But the French were at war with the British. The French government needed money.

In the early 1800s, large areas of North America had not yet been explored by US citizens.

And France was not sure it could defend Louisiana if the British attacked. So, France offered to sell the territory to the United States for $15 million.

US President Thomas Jefferson was thrilled. He was eager for the United States to expand to the west. In April 1803, the two nations signed the Louisiana Purchase Treaty. Louisiana was now part of the United States. The territory covered 828,000 square miles (2,144,500 sq km). It reached all the way to the Rocky Mountains. Many different American Indian nations lived in this territory. But few settlers knew what the area was like.

Jefferson wanted to learn about the land and the people who lived there. He asked his personal secretary, Meriwether Lewis, to lead an **expedition**. This group would travel through the new territory and explore it.

LEWIS AND CLARK'S JOURNEY

BRITISH TERRITORY

FORT CLATSOP

MARIAS RIVER

COLUMBIA RIVER

GREAT FALLS

YELLOWSTONE RIVER

FORT MANDAN

SNAKE RIVER

MISSOURI RIVER

PHILADELPHIA

WASHINGTON, DC

SPANISH TERRITORY

LOUISIANA TERRITORY

ST. LOUIS

OHIO RIVER

UNITED STATES

MISSISSIPPI RIVER

LEWIS AND CLARK'S ROUTE

N
W E
S

To prepare for the journey, Lewis went to Philadelphia, Pennsylvania. Experts there taught him about **botany**, **navigation**, mapmaking, and medicine. Lewis realized he needed a partner. He wrote a letter to his friend William Clark. Lewis and Clark had served in the army together. Lewis asked Clark to help command the expedition. Clark accepted eagerly.

Then Lewis and Clark made careful preparations. They had a large boat built specially for the voyage. They purchased two other boats as well. Lewis bought guns, clothing, medicine, and scientific instruments.

Lewis (left) and Clark (right) co-led the expedition.

Lewis and Clark **recruited** a group of approximately 40 men to join them. The group included a man named York, who was enslaved by Clark. The group expected to meet American Indians during the journey. For this reason, they brought gifts and items to trade.

CHAPTER 2

SETTING OUT

After several months of planning, everything was ready. On May 14, 1804, the expedition set out from a camp near St. Louis, Missouri. The men sailed their boats north along the Missouri River. Whenever they stopped to rest, the men explored the lands around the river. They found many animals to hunt.

This replica shows what the expedition's keelboat looked like.

Some, such as bison, were familiar. But many were new to the explorers. These animals included prairie dogs, bighorn sheep, and grizzly bears.

Both Lewis and Clark kept journals during the journey. They described the plants and animals they saw. They also recorded the **topography** of the land. Clark drew maps, too.

Members of the Mandan and Arikara communities watched as the group made its way across the territories where they lived. These American Indians met the explorers. Lewis and Clark gave them flags, medals, clothes, and tobacco as **tokens** of friendship. The explorers

The explorers met several different American Indian nations during their journey.

spoke admiringly of President Jefferson. They called him the "great father" in Washington, DC.

The explorers met the Mandan people in late October. Winter was coming. So, Lewis and Clark built a fort near the Mandans. They called it Fort Mandan.

Trade with the Mandans made it possible for the explorers to survive the winter.

The men cut down trees to build wooden huts. Despite the hard work, everyone found ways to relax. Sometimes one man played the violin. Everyone would dance late into the night.

At the Mandan camp, Lewis and Clark met Toussaint Charbonneau. He was a French Canadian fur trapper and trader. Charbonneau lived among the Hidatsa people. He introduced the explorers to his wife, Sacagawea. She was a member of the Shoshone tribe.

Charbonneau and Sacagawea each spoke several languages. They offered to join the expedition as translators. Lewis and Clark agreed. That winter, Sacagawea gave birth to a baby boy. He became the youngest member of the expedition.

During the winter, Lewis and Clark studied their maps and made plans. By the time spring arrived, they were ready to continue their journey. In April 1805, they said goodbye to Fort Mandan and continued west. They hoped to travel all the way to the Pacific Ocean.

SACAGAWEA

Sacagawea was the only woman in the expedition. Without her, the men risked being mistaken for a war party. But women did not travel with war parties. Her presence made it clear that the men did not plan to attack.

Sacagawea helped the expedition in many other ways. She spoke Shoshone and Hidatsa. Her husband Charbonneau spoke Hidatsa and French. Together, they helped the explorers communicate with American Indian tribes. In addition, Sacagawea's quick thinking helped the explorers. Once, a gust of wind tipped one of the boats. Important supplies fell into the Yellowstone River. Sacagawea jumped into action. She caught most of the packages before they sank or floated away. In his journal, Lewis said her "fortitude and resolution" prevented a disaster.

When the expedition met the Shoshone, Sacagawea saw her brother Cameahwait for the first time in years.

Later, the group met the Shoshone. Clark wrote that Sacagawea "danced for the joyful sight." The chief of the Shoshone was her brother. When Sacagawea was young, another tribe had captured her. She had been separated from her family for many years. But now they were reunited.

CHAPTER 3

TOWARD THE PACIFIC COAST

More than a year after setting out, Lewis and Clark's expedition arrived at the Great Falls of the Missouri River. These spectacular waterfalls were too dangerous to cross by boat. Instead, the explorers carried everything they had around the falls. This process took 12 days. It was slow, tough going.

Carrying boats over land is called portaging.

Sacagawea helped guide the expedition over the Rocky Mountains.

The ground was thorny and uneven. This made it difficult to walk. Mosquitoes bit the explorers, too. One day, some of the men were caught in a flash flood. Fortunately, none were harmed.

Finally, the expedition reached the Rocky Mountains. To cross the mountains, the explorers needed horses to carry their supplies. Sacagawea was able to help. She convinced the Shoshones to trade with the explorers for the horses. The Shoshones also helped find someone to guide the explorers over the mountains.

The **trek** through the Rocky Mountains took more than a month. It was very difficult. Everyone suffered from the cold. And nobody had enough to eat. The local Nez Perce people helped the explorers. They gave them buffalo meat, berries, roots, and dried salmon. The explorers were not used to eating some of these things. The unfamiliar food made them ill. But it kept them from starving.

The explorers sailed down the Columbia River to the Pacific Ocean.

By now, the explorers had crossed the Louisiana Territory. They kept going west toward the Pacific Ocean. They got their first glimpse of this vast ocean on November 15, 1805.

The explorers spent the next several days exploring the areas near the coast. But it would soon be winter. Lewis and

Clark decided to stay where they were until spring. They built a camp near the coast. The local Clatsop people welcomed them warmly. In honor of the Clatsops, the explorers named their winter **quarters** Fort Clatsop.

ASSISTANCE ALONG THE WAY

The explorers passed through the lands of several American Indian nations. Without their help, the explorers could not have survived.

CHAPTER 4

THE JOURNEY HOME

When spring came, the explorers left Fort Clatsop. They had crossed the continent. Now they were ready to return home. Slowly, the explorers made their way east. They climbed back over the Rocky Mountains. But there was still so much land they had not explored. So, Lewis and Clark decided to split up.

This replica of Fort Clatsop shows what the explorers' winter quarters were like.

Clark's group followed the Yellowstone River, which flows into the Missouri River.

They formed two groups. Lewis led one group. Clark led the other.

The groups took different routes for part of the journey. Clark's group explored the area around the Yellowstone River. Lewis's group traveled north along the Missouri River. They came into contact with members of the Blackfeet nation, who were not pleased to see them.

A fight broke out, and two Blackfeet were killed. This was the only fight between the explorers and American Indians during the whole journey.

Lewis's group and Clark's group met up again on August 12, 1806. Together, they made the final part of the journey. They traveled back down the Missouri River, the same way they had come.

The explorers made it back to St. Louis, Missouri, on September 23, 1806. They had been gone for two years, four months, and ten days. They had traveled nearly 8,000 miles (12,875 km). One group member had died of a burst appendix. But everyone else returned safe and sound.

This sketch from Clark's journal shows the leaves of an evergreen shrub.

After they returned, Lewis and Clark traveled to Washington, DC. They told President Jefferson about what they had seen. They brought **specimens** of several plants and animals. Scientists studied these specimens to learn more about the wildlife west of the Mississippi River.

Several years later, in 1814, Lewis and Clark's journals were published. More people could read their notes and see their drawings.

Lewis and Clark's journey paved the way for more people to settle in the Louisiana Territory. Within a few years, whole families were traveling west to the new land. They founded villages and towns. But they also disrupted the way of life for many American Indian nations. The settlers brought diseases with them. Many American Indians died as a result.

The United States continued to grow. Several US presidents encouraged settlers to move west. By the mid-1800s, the United States stretched all the way across North America.

FOCUS ON
THE LEWIS AND CLARK EXPEDITION

Write your answers on a separate piece of paper.

1. Write a paragraph summarizing the main accomplishments of the Lewis and Clark expedition.

2. If Lewis and Clark had asked you to join their expedition, would you have gone? Why or why not?

3. Who joined the expedition as a translator?

    A. Thomas Jefferson

    B. Meriwether Lewis

    C. Sacagawea

4. Why did the explorers split up during their return journey?

    A. so they could return home more quickly

    B. so they could explore more of the land

    C. so they could go around a flooded area

Answer key on page 32.

GLOSSARY

botany
The study of plants.

expedition
A journey or voyage made with a specific goal in mind.

navigation
Skills or strategies used to find one's way while traveling.

quarters
Places where people live, especially as part of a job.

recruited
Found new members to join a group or activity.

specimens
Examples of individual animals or plants that show what the entire group of animals or plants is like.

territory
An area of land or a region of a country.

tokens
Things that are given as signs or reminders.

topography
The surface and natural features (such as forests, lakes, and rivers) of an area of land.

trek
A journey that is slow and often difficult.

TO LEARN MORE

BOOKS

Blashfield, Jean F. *The Amazing Lewis and Clark Expedition*. North Mankato, MN: Capstone Press, 2018.

Micklos, John, Jr. *Discovering the West: The Expedition of Lewis and Clark*. North Mankato, MN: Capstone Press, 2015.

St. George, Judith. *What Was the Lewis and Clark Expedition?* New York: Penguin Random House, 2014.

NOTE TO EDUCATORS

Visit **www.focusreaders.com** to find lesson plans, activities, links, and other resources related to this title.

INDEX

Answer Key: 1. Answers will vary; 2. Answers will vary; 3. C; 4. B